Best Wishes — CAS '73

Canadian
Play
Series

David
Freeman | **Creeps**

University of Toronto Press

Canadian Play Series
General Editor: Jack Gray

ISBN 0-8020-6144-3

Printed in Canada

To my Father

PETE   I've been weaving that stupid rug beside that
           hot radiator every day now for three months.
           And what has it got me? A big fat zero.

SAUNDERS   (Off) Boys! What's going on in there? If you
            don't come out this minute I'm coming in.

   SAM   We dare you!

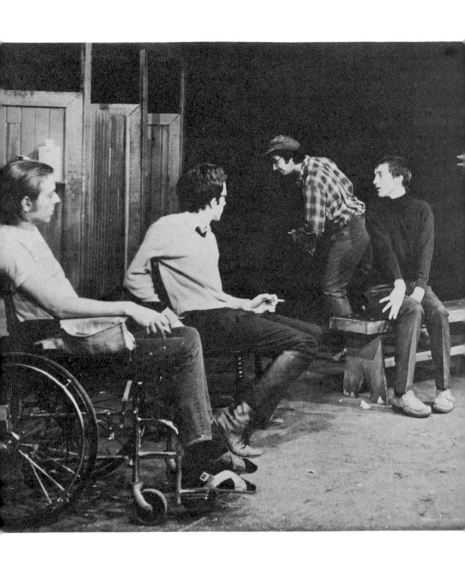

PETE   Jesus Christ, Jim, Puffo the Clown!

CARSON   You leave that bottle alone. I want you all
          out of here.

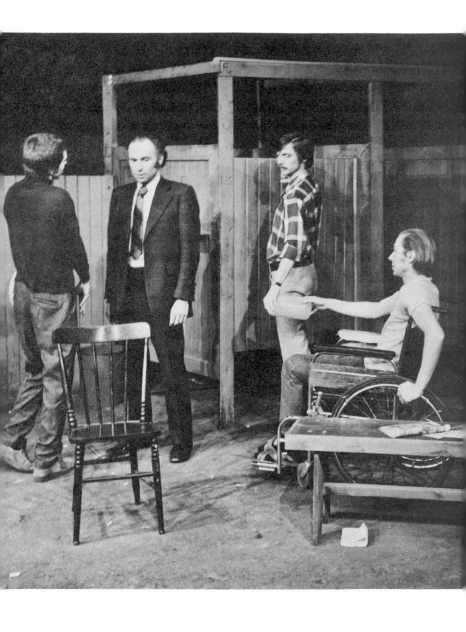

Creeps was first presented at The Factory Lab
Theatre, Toronto, on February 5, 1970, with
the following cast:

           Pete - Victor Sutton
            Jim - Robert Coltri
            Sam - Steven Whistance-Smith
            Tom - Frank Moore
        Michael - Len Sedun
       Saunders - Kay Griffin
         Carson - Bert Adkins
           Girl - Christina Zorro
       Shriners - Bernard Bomers, Mark Freeborn

Directed by Bill Glassco
Designed by Peter Kolisnyk

This revised version of Creeps was first
presented at Tarragon Theatre, Toronto, on
October 5, 1971, with the following cast:

           Pete - Victor Sutton
            Jim - Robert Coltri
            Sam - Steven Whistance-Smith
            Tom - Frank Moore
        Michael - Len Sedun
       Saunders - Josephine Smith
         Carson - Richard Davidson
           Girl - Robin Cameron
       Shriners - John Candy, Charles Northcote

Directed by Bill Glassco
Designed by Peter Kolisnyk

The actor playing the role of Michael also plays
the Chef, Puffo The Clown, and the Carnival
Barker in the three Shriner sequences.

The play is set in the washroom of a sheltered
workshop for cerebral palsy victims. A
"sheltered workshop" is a place where disabled
people can go and work at their own pace without
the pressure of the competitive outside world.
Its aim is not to provide a living wage for the
C.P., but rather to occupy his idle hours.

SOME NOTES ON THE CHARACTERS' MOVEMENTS

Each actor taking a role of one of the charac-
ters with cerebral palsy is faced, as the
character, with major physical problems, the
practical solution of which is paramount to a
successful rendering of the play. It is to be
noted that there are many kinds of spasticity,
and each actor should base his movements on
one of these. There can be no substitute for
the first-hand observation of these physical
problems, and one might even suggest that the
play not be attempted if opportunities for such
first-hand observation are not available. These
notes indicate the approach taken by the actors
in the original production.

PETE
The actor in the original production developed
a way of speaking that is common to many
spastics. The effort required to speak causes
a distortion of the facial muscles. The actor
was able to achieve this by thrusting the jaw
forward, and letting the lower jaw hang.
Whatever speech problem is adopted for this
role, no actor should attempt it unless he has
an opportunity for first hand observation.

The deformed hand was not held rigid in one
position. The actor used the hand for many
things, keeping the fist clenched and employing the fingers in a clawlike manner.

JIM
The actor walked with his knees almost touching,
feet apart, back bent much of the time, using
his arms more than any other part of his body
for balance.

SAM
Sam is a diaplegic, his body dead from the
waist down (except for his genitals). He is in
a wheelchair. The problem for this actor was to
find how to make the wheelchair an extension of
his body.

TOM
The actor walked with one hip thrust out to the
side. Forward motion always began with the foot
of the other leg, rising up on the toe, and
then thrusting downward on the heel. His arms
were held in front of him, his fingers splayed,
upper arms and shoulders constantly being
employed for balance.

MICHAEL
The actor always staggered, his head lolling,
his body very loose, constantly on the edge of
falling. He fell, or collapsed, rather than sat,
and grinned most of the time. He too had a
speech problem, very slurred, not employing the
facial muscles like Pete.

A men's washroom in a sheltered workshop.
The hall leading to the washroom is visible.
In the washroom are two urinals and two stalls.
A chair is set against one of the stalls and
there is a bench.

When the lights go up one of the stalls is
occupied. Michael, a mentally retarded C.P.
of about eighteen, comes along the hall,
enters the door of the washroom, and starts
flushing the toilets, beginning with the
urinals. He comes to the occupied stall and
knocks on the door.

PETE   Who is it?

THELMA   (An offstage voice. It is important that this
           voice be spastic, but that what she is saying
           always be clear) I need a priest!

           Michael chuckles to himself, does not answer.
           Meanwhile Tom has entered, walking in a sway
           and stagger motion. Having observed the game
           Michael is playing on Pete, he ushers Michael
           out, then sits in the chair up against the
           stall occupied by Pete. Pete drops his pack of
           cigarettes

TOM   (Disguising his voice) Hey, Pete, you dropped
           your cigarettes. (Pause. A comic book falls)
           Hey, Pete, you dropped your comic book.

           Pete's pants drop to the floor

TOM   (His own voice) Hey, Pete, you dropped your
           pants.

PETE   That you, Tom?

TOM   Course it's me. Who were you expecting, Woody
           the Pecker?

PETE   Why didn't you answer?

TOM   When?

1

PETE	Didn't you knock on the door just now?
TOM	No.
PETE	Must have been Michael flushing toilets.
TOM	Doing his thing.
PETE	He wants to be toilet flushing champion of the world.
TOM	Well at least he's not like some lazy bastards who sit on their ass all day reading comic books.
PETE	I'm on strike. They only pay me seventy-five cents a week. I'm worth eighty.
TOM	You're always on strike.
PETE	How many boxes did you fold today, smart ass?
TOM	Oh, about two hundred. How's the rug?
PETE	Fucking rug. I wish to hell she'd put me on something else. At least for a day or two. It's getting to be a real drag.
TOM	Yeah, that's the way I feel about those boxes.
THELMA	I need a priest! Get me a priest!
TOM	(Wearily) Oh, God.
PETE	Old Thelma kind of gets on your nerves, doesn't she?
TOM	Yeah.
THELMA	Someone get me a priest!
TOM	Pete, I gotta talk to you about something.
PETE	Okay, shoot.
TOM	No, I'll wait till you're out of the can.

Knock at the door

SAM	Open up! (Pause) Who's in there?

Tom moves to open the door

SAM	Come on, for Chrissake.
TOM	All right, hang on.

With difficulty Tom gets the door open. Sam
wheels by him into the washroom

2

TOM   Wanna take a leak, Sam?

SAM   No, I wanna join the circle jerk. Where's Pete?

PETE In here.

SAM   Well, well, Pete is actually using the shithouse to take a shit.

PETE Okay, Sam, knock it off.

Pause

TOM   (To Sam) How are you making out with the blocks?

SAM   Screw the blocks. You know how many of those fuckin' things I done today? Two. Do you know why? Because that half-ass physical therapist...

TOM   Physio.

SAM   Physio, physical, what the fuck's the difference? They're all after my body. She keeps making me do the same damn blocks over again. "That's not good enough," she says. "Get the edges smoother," she says. (Pointing to his crotch) Take a bite of this.

PETE (Flushing the toilet) She can be a pretty miserable old cunt at times.

SAM   All the time. How's the rug, Pete?

PETE That thing.

TOM   I told him, he's never gonna finish it sitting in the john all day.

PETE (Emerging from the stall) I've been weaving that stupid rug beside that hot radiator every day now for three months. And what has it got me? A big fat zero.

SAM   That's because you're a lazy bugger. You know what that stupid idiot who runs this dump says about you.

PETE Yeah, I know. "Pete, if you worked in my factory, you wouldn't last a day..."

TOM   "But since you're a helpless cripple, I'll let you work in my workshop..."

SAM   "For free!"

PETE And the government will give me a pension, just for breathing.

3

TOM And the Rotary and the Shriners will provide
     hot dogs and ice cream.

SAM And remember, boys, "If they won't do it..."

ALL "Nobody else will!"

     Blackout. Circus music and bright lights. Enter
     two Shriners, a girl (Miss Cerebral Palsy) in a
     white bathing suit, and a chef. They dance
     around the boys, posing for pictures, blowing
     noisemakers, and generally molesting them in
     the name of charity. The chef stuffs hot dogs
     into their hands. They exit, the music fades,
     the light returns to normal. The boys throw
     their hot dogs over the back of the set

PETE Sometimes I wonder how I ever got myself into
      this.

TOM   Good question, Pete. How did you?

PETE Another time, Tom, another time.

THELMA I need a priest!

PETE What's this big piece of news you have to tell
      me?

TOM   It doesn't matter.

PETE Come on, Tom, crap it out.

TOM   It's okay, forget it.

PETE I postponed my shit for this.

TOM   That's your problem.

SAM   Hey, I bet he's gonna get laid and he doesn't
      know what to do.

PETE Well the first thing he better learn is how to
      get undressed faster.

TOM   Very funny.

PETE What's the matter? This place still getting you
      down?

TOM   Yeah, I can't hack it much longer.

SAM   Can't hack what?

TOM   Everything. Folding boxes, the Spastic Club,
      Thelma, the whole bit.

4

PETE   How's the art coming?

TOM   Didn't you hear me?

PETE   Sure I heard you. You said you couldn't hack
       folding boxes. Well I can't hack weaving that
       goddamn rug. So how's the art?

TOM   Screw the art. I don't want to talk about art.

PETE   Okay.

SAM   Chickentracks.

TOM   What's that?

SAM   Chickentracks. That's what you paint, Tom.
       Chickentracks.

TOM   I paint abstract. I know to some ignorant
       assholes it looks like chickentracks...

SAM   Listen, Rembrandt, anything you ever tried to
       paint always looked like shit warmed over, so
       you try to cover it up by calling it an
       abstract. But it's chickenshit and you know it.

TOM   You wouldn't know the difference between a tree
       and a telephone pole, Sam.

SAM   There isn't any difference. A dog'll piss on
       both of them.

TOM   And you'll piss on anything, won't you?

PETE   Okay, Tom, cool it.

TOM   Why the fuck should I cool it? This prick's
       attacking my art.

PETE   You shouldn't take yourself so seriously.

TOM   Oh, do forgive me, gentlemen. I took myself
       seriously. (Getting up) I shall go to Miss
       Saunders and insist she castrate me.

       He starts for the door

SAM   Castrate what?

PETE   Where are you going?

TOM   Where does it look like?

PETE   Dammit, Tom, come on back and stop acting like
       an idiot.

5

TOM   Why should I? Whenever anyone tries to talk serious around here, you guys turn it into a joke.

PETE   Nobody's making a joke.

SAM   Look, Tom, even if you do have talent, which I seriously doubt, what good is it to you? You know bloody well they're not going to let you use it.

TOM   Who's they, Sam?

SAM   The Rotary, the Shriners, the Kiwanis, the creeps who run this dump. In fact, the whole goddamn world. Look, if we start making it, they won't have anyone to be embarrassed about.

PETE   Come on, Sam, there's always the blacks.

TOM   And the Indians.

SAM   Yeah, but we're more of a challenge. You can always throw real shit at a black man or an Indian, but at us you're only allowed to throw pityshit. And pityshit ain't visible.

TOM   I think you're stretching it just a bit.

SAM   The only way you're going to get to use that talent of yours, Tom, is to give someone's ass an extra big juicy kiss. And you ought to know by now how brilliantly that works for some people round here.

TOM   You mean Harris?

SAM   If the shoe fits.

TOM   You lay off Jim, 'cause if you'd had the same opportunity you'd have done the same thing.

SAM   So now he licks stamps in the office on a weekly salary, and he's president of the Spastic Club. Whoopee!

TOM   (To Pete) Are you going to talk to me or not?

       Jim enters and goes to the urinal. He is surprised to see Tom. His walk is slow and shaky, almost a drunken stagger

SAM   Here's Mommy's boy now.

       Pause

6

PETE   Things slack in the office, Jim?

JIM   Naw, I just thought I might be missing something.

SAM   Oh you're sweet. Isn't he sweet? I love him.

PETE   Cigarette?

JIM   No thanks, I'm trying to give them up.

        He flushes the urinal

SAM   Shouldn't be difficult. Giving up is what you do best.

JIM   Aren't you guys worried about getting caught? (To Pete) You know you've been in here for over an hour.

SAM   Shit time. Push me into the crapper, will ya, Pete.

PETE   Saunders won't come in here.

JIM   She might, Pete. Remember Rick and Stanley.

PETE   I do, but I'm not Rick and Stanley.

TOM   Jim, that story's horseshit. Those guys weren't queer.

SAM   (From the stall) Sure they were queer. Why do you think they always sat together at lunch, for Chrissake?

PETE   I'll never forget the day she caught them in here necking. Screamed her bloody head off. (To Tom) Of course the reason she gave for separating them was that they were talking too much and not getting their work done. Right, Jim? (Jim says nothing) No, Saunders won't come in here now. Not after a shock like that.

SAM   Maybe not, but she might send Cinderella to check up on us. How 'bout it, Princess?

JIM   Why would I do a thing like that?

PETE   Then why did you come in?

JIM   Is this washroom exclusive or something?

TOM   It's not that, Jim. It's just that you haven't been to one of our bull sessions for a long time. Not since your promotion.

JIM   I already told you. I just wanted to see if I was missing something.

7

SAM	You are. Your balls.

Knock at the door

SAUNDERS	Jim! What's happening in there? I haven't got all day.

Silence. Pete and Tom look at Jim

JIM	Okay, so she asked me. But I didn't come in here to spy.
SAM	Well move your ass, Romeo. You heard what the lady said, she can't wait all day.
SAUNDERS	Jim?
SAM	Bye-bye.
SAUNDERS	Jim, are you there?

Jim moves towards the door

TOM	Wait, Jim, you don't have to go.
SAM	Dammit, let the fucker go. His mommy wants him.
PETE	Shut up, Sam.
SAM	I wasn't talking to you.
TOM	Why don't you stay for a while?
PETE	Yeah, tell old tight-cunt you're on the can or something.

He grabs Jim and pulls him away from the door

SAUNDERS	Jim Harris! Do you hear me!?

Pete signals to Jim to answer

JIM	Yes, Miss Saunders, I hear you. But I'm on the toilet at the moment.
SAUNDERS	What are you doing on the toilet?
PETE	(At the door) He's taking a shit. What do you do on the toilet?
SAUNDERS	If you boys aren't back to work in five minutes I'm reporting you to Mr. Carson.

She walks back down the hall

8

SAM   Once upon a time, boys, there was a boudingy
bird, and the cry of the boudingy went like
this...

TOM & (In falsetto, forestalling Sam) Suck my
PETE   boudingy!

Silence while Pete listens at the door

JIM   I could use that cigarette now.

PETE (Bringing him one) Thought you were trying to
quit.

JIM   I am.

Pause

TOM   Jim, why did you lie?

JIM   I did not lie. Saunders saw me coming in, and
she thought I might remind you that you'd been
in here a long time. That's all.

TOM   Then why didn't you say so when Sam asked you?

SAM   Because he's so used to telling lies, if
anyone said he was spastic, he'd deny it.

TOM   Will ya shut up, Sam.

JIM   That's okay. Sam didn't care for me when I was
sanding blocks with him.

SAM   Pete, push that chair in here, will you?

JIM   Now that he thinks I've gone over to the other
side, he's got even less reason to like me.

SAM   Listen, Princess, nobody likes a white nigger.

TOM   What's that mean, Sam?

PETE (As he holds the chair for Sam) Why don't you
use a bedpan?

SAM   Why do you think, dummy? Because my ass begins
to look like the other side of the moon. (By
now he is off the toilet and back in the chair)
All right, all right.

He wheels backwards out of the stall

JIM   Well, Sam?

9

SAM   Well what, stooge?

JIM   What do you mean, white nigger?

SAM   Well since you're all so fired fuckin' dyin' to
        know, I'll tell you. You finished high school,
        didn't you?

JIM   Yes.

SAM   And you went to university?

JIM   Yes.

SAM   And you got a degree?

JIM   So?

SAM   Well, you went to university. You wrote all that
        crap for the paper about how shitty it was to be
        handicapped in this country. Then what do you
        do? You come running down here and kiss the
        first ass you see. That's what I mean by being
        a white nigger, and that's what fuckin' well
        pisses me off.

JIM   All right, Sam, now you listen to me. I still
        believe everything I wrote, and I intend to
        act on it. But you can't change things until
        you're in a position to call the shots. And
        you don't get there without being nice to
        people. By the way, what are you doing about
        it? All I ever get from you is bitch, bitch,
        bitch!

SAM   I got every fuckin' right to bitch. You expect
        me to sand blocks and put up with the pityshit
        routine for ninety-nine years waiting for you
        to get your ass into a position of power? Fuck
        you, buddy! You give me a choice and I'll stop
        bitching.

TOM   Now look who's taking himself seriously.

SAM   (To Tom and Pete) What do you guys know about
        the bullshit I put up with? My old lady, now
        get this, my old lady has devoted her entire
        goddamn life to martyrdom. And my old man, you
        ever met my old man? Ever seen him give me one
        of his "Where have I failed?" looks? Wait'll
        ya hear what happened last night. He invited
        his boss over for dinner, and you know where
        the old bugger wanted me to eat? In the kitchen.

First I told him to go screw the dog -- that's about his style -- and then, at the height of the festivities, just when everything was going real nice for daddy, I puked all over the table.

TOM   Charming.

SAM   It was beautiful. Stuck my finger down my throat and out it all came: roast beef, mashed potatoes, peas, olives. There was a real abstract painting, Tom. You should have seen the look on his boss's face. Be a long time before he gives at the office again.

        Michael enters. During the ensuing dialogue he attempts to flush the urinals, but is stopped by signals from Pete

JIM   You know, Sam, you amaze me. You say you don't want to wait ninety-nine years, but you're happy if you can set us back a few. A stunt like that doesn't make Carson's job any easier.

PETE   Okay, Timmy, you're not addressing the Spastic Club.

SAM   Piss on Carson! He doesn't give a shit about us and you know it.

JIM   I don't know it. I don't know what his motives are. But I do know he's trying to help us.

PETE   His motives are to keep the niggers in their place.

SAM   Yeah, by getting Uncle Timmy here to watch over them.

TOM   (To Sam and Pete) What are you guys, the resident hypocrites? Look, no one twists your arm to go to those Spastic Club meetings. No one forces those hot dogs down your throat.

PETE   Sure, we take them. Why not? They're free. Why look a gift horse in the mouth? But at least we don't kiss ass.

JIM   No, you let me do it for you. (Slight pause) But that's beside the point. The point is that Carson does care about what happens to us.

SAM   He does?

11

JIM	You're darn right he does.
SAM	You ever been over to his house for dinner?
JIM	Yes.
SAM	Ever been back?
JIM	No.
SAM	In other words, you got your token dinner, and now you only see him at Spastic Club meetings and here at the workshop?
JIM	That's not true. He comes to my place sometimes, doesn't he, Tom?
TOM	Yeah, but what about all those times your mother invited him for dinner and he cancelled out at the last minute?
JIM	So? That doesn't prove anything.
SAM	It proves a helluva lot to me.

Michael pokes Pete on the shoulder

PETE	What is it, Michael?
MICHAEL	Cigarette, please.
PETE	Okay, Michael, but smoke it this time, don't eat it. Last time everyone accused me of trying to poison you.

Banging at the door

SAUNDERS	Boys! What's going on in there? If you don't come out this minute I'm coming in.
SAM	We dare you!
TOM	Shut up, Sam.
SAUNDERS	What was that?
PETE	Nothing, Miss Saunders. Sam just said, "We hear you."
SAUNDERS	Oh no he didn't. I know what he said. He said, "We dare you."
PETE	Well Christ, if you already knew, what the fuck did you ask for? (To himself) Stupid bitch!
SAUNDERS	Jim. What's happening in there? Are they doing something they shouldn't?

12

SAM	Yeah, we're pissing through our noses!
JIM	Cut it out, Sam. No, Tom and Pete are on the toilets, and I'm holding the bottle for Sam.
SAM	Hey, that hurts! Don't **pull** so hard, you idiot!
SAUNDERS	(Nonplussed) Well hurry up, and stop fooling around. I can't wait on you all day.

She starts down the hallway, stops when she hears

SAM	(To the door) That's it, Pete, no more blowjobs for cigarettes! Jim, take your hands off me, I've only got one! Michael, don't use your teeth! Christ, I've never seen so many queers in one place. I could open a fruit stand!

Saunders listens, horrified, then runs off down the hall. Michael sits on the floor and begins to eat the cigarette. The laughter subsides

PETE	I think she left.

Pause

TOM	Do I finally get to say something?
PETE	Oh yeah, where were we? You couldn't hack folding boxes.
TOM	Or the Spastic Club.
PETE	Or the Spastic Club.
TOM	Or Thelma.
PETE	Or Thelma.
TOM	Pete.
PETE	What's the matter now?
TOM	Cochran, for once in your life, will you be serious?
PETE	I'm fucking serious.
SAM	It's the only way to fuck.
PETE	If I was any more serious, I'd be dead. I wish to hell you'd get on with it, Tom.

Pause

TOM   You guys ever read a story called "Premature
            Burial"?

            Sam and Jim shake their heads

PETE   What comic was it in?

TOM   Edgar Allen Poe.

PETE   Oh.

TOM   Anyway, it's about this guy who has this
            sickness that puts him into a coma every so
            often. And he's scared as hell someone's going
            to mistake him and bury him alive. Well, that's
            the way I feel about this workshop. It's like
            I'm at the bottom of a grave yelling "I'm
            alive! I am alive!" But they don't hear me.
            They just keep shovelling in the dirt.

THELMA   I need a priest!

JIM   Tom, if you really feel that way, you ought to
            talk to Carson.

TOM   Oh, fuck off.

JIM   He's not an idiot, you know.

PETE   Tom, you want to know what I think? I think you
            should stop reading junk like Edgar Allen Poe.
            You take that stuff too seriously.

SAM   Pete's right. You should stick to your regular
            diet.

TOM   What's that crack supposed to mean?

SAM   It's sticking out of your back pocket, sexy.

            Tom reaches round and removes a book from his
            pocket

TOM   (Tossing it to Sam) Here, Sam, why don't you
            take it for a while? Maybe it'll shut you up.

SAM   (As he flicks through the book) Hey, he's got
            the dirty parts underlined in red.

PETE   Read some.

SAM   (Reading) "Nothing like a nice yellow banana,"
            she said aloud. It touched every sensitive area
            of her pussy. Tears came to her eyes in shots
            of violent lust. Then her movements began to
            increase and she spliced herself repeatedly...

            14

TOM   That's enough, Sam.

SAM   The thick banana swirled in her cunt like a
       battering ram. She grasped it hard and shoved
       it faster and faster. Then she sat up, still
       gorged with the banana...

TOM   I said, that's enough!

       He gets up and moves to take the book away from
       Sam

SAM   (Who has not stopped reading) It hit high up
       against the walls of her wet cunt. She could
       move whichever way she liked. "Oh, shit, this
       is juicy," she said aloud. The reflection she
       saw in the mirror was ludicrous and made her
       even more hot. "Oh you big banana, fuck me!..."

       Tom grabs the book

PETE   Wait. I want to find out about the banana split.

TOM   If you're so hot about the banana, you can have
       the goddamn book.

       He gives it to him

SAM   It'll only cost you a nickel, Pete, it's under-
       lined.

TOM   Okay. So I get a charge out of dirty books.
       What does that make me, a creep?

SAM   Well at least I don't pretend to be something
       I'm not. I don't work myself up during office
       hours.

TOM   No, you just do it at picnics.

SAM   What about a goddamn picnic?

JIM   Come on, Sam, you remember the Rotarian's
       daughter.

SAM   So I remember a Rotarian's daughter. What now?

PETE   She was sitting beside you and you were feeling
       her up like crazy, that's what now.

SAM   If the silly little fart is stupid enough to
       let me, why not?

JIM   You were making a bloody spectacle of yourself.

15

SAM	Love is where you find it.
PETE	Yeah, but with you working her over like that, I could hardly keep my mind on the three-legged race. Didn't she even say anything?
SAM	Nope, she just sat there. Smiled a lot.
THELMA	I need a priest! (Pause)
JIM	There's a girl who isn't smiling, is she, Sam?
SAM	Shut up, Harris.
THELMA	Get me a priest!
TOM	Ever since I've been here, Thelma's always calling for a priest. How come?
PETE	Sam knows.
SAM	Yeah, well mind your own business.
THELMA	Someone get me a priest!
SAM	(Screams, overlapping Thelma) Dry up, you stupid fuckin' broad!
PETE	Why don't you go comfort her, Sam? You used to be pretty good at comforting old Thelma.
JIM	Yeah, you couldn't keep your hands off her.
SAM	What's the matter, were ya jealous, princess?
TOM	Hey, I'd like to know what the hell's going on.
PETE	This was before your time, Tom. Thelma was all right then. Cute kid, as a matter of fact. Until old horney here got his hands on her and drove her off her rocker.
SAM	That's a fuckin' lie. The doctors said it wasn't my fault.
JIM	They only told you that to make it easy for you.
SAM	Look, it wasn't my fault.
JIM	What you did sure didn't help any.
SAM	Well why bring it up now?
PETE	Because we're sick and tired of having you put everybody down. It's time someone put you down for a change.
TOM	Well, what did he do? Will you please tell me?

16

PETE   From the day Thelma got here, Sam was after her like a hot stud. Being so nice to her, and then coming in here and bragging how she was letting him feel her up, and bragging how he was gonna fuck the ass off her soon.

THELMA   I want a priest!

PETE   Maybe you've heard, Tom, that Thelma's parents are religious. I don't just mean they're devout, they're real dingalings about it. Like they believe Thelma's the way she is because of some great sin they've committed. Like that. Anyway, she was home in bed one weekend with a cold, and Sam went over to visit her, and her parents weren't out of the room two seconds when Sam was into her pants.

SAM   That's another goddamn lie. It didn't happen that way.

PETE   Okay, so it took a full minute. Don't quibble over details.

SAM   Look I didn't mean for anything to happen that day. What do you think I am, stupid? In the first place, she had a cold, and in the second place, her parents were out on the goddamn porch. I just wanted to talk. She started fooling around, trying to grab my cannon and everything. Naturally I get a hard-on. What am I supposed to do? Silly little bitch! We were just going real good when she changed her mind. That's one helluva time to exercise her woman's prerogative, isn't it? Anyway, we...she fell out of bed. In a few seconds in come Mommy and Daddy. They thought I'd fallen out of my chair or something. Well, there I am in bed with my joint waving merrily in the breeze, and Thelma's on the floor minus her P.J.'s, and all hell broke loose. You'd have thought they'd never seen a cock before. The old man, he bounced me out of bed along the floor and into the hallway. The old lady, she dragged Thelma up behind. Then they held us up in front of a little Jesus statue and asked it to forgive us 'cause we didn't know what we were doing. (Pause) The doctors said it wasn't my fault.

JIM   They were only feeling sorry for a horny cripple in a wheelchair.

17

PETE   Yeah, but we all know the truth, don't we Sam?

SAM   (Overlapping) Why don't you shut the fuck up,
           Cochran!

JIM   Hey Pete, remember how Thelma used to dress
           before Sam put his rod to her? So pretty.

TOM   Okay, guys, knock it off.

PETE   Yeah, but that's all over now. Now she only
           wears black and brown, and everything's covered,
           right up to the neck.

JIM   She used to laugh a lot too.

TOM   That's enough!

THELMA   I need a priest!

MICHAEL   (Sing-song) Thelma needs a priest. Thelma needs
           a priest.

SAM   Fuck off! Piece of shit!

           Sam goes for Michael, who is sitting on the
           floor, and hits out at him. Michael is
           surprised, but hits back. To stop the fight,
           Pete grabs Sam's chair from behind. Sam then
           lashes out at Pete. At the same time, Jim and
           Tom go to rescue Michael. Jim falls while Tom
           tries to get Michael's attention away from
           Sam. Throughout the commotion Michael continues
           to yell, "Thelma needs a priest." Finally, Sam
           wheels angrily away and Pete helps Jim up

TOM   (At one of the urinals) Hey, Michael, look, a
           cockroach. Big fat one.

           Michael sees the cockroach and gets very
           excited. Pete, Tom, and Jim gather round him
           at the urinal

PETE   Hey, Sam, there's livestock in the pisser.

TOM   (To Michael) Why don't you use your ray gun and
           disintegrate it?

MICHAEL   What ray gun? I got no ray gun.

SAM   Yes, you have. That thing between your legs.
           It's a ray gun.

           Michael looks down and makes the connection

MICHAEL   (Delighted) I disintegrate it. I disintegrate
           it all up.

           He turns into the urinal

SAM   You do that.

           Saunders returns and knocks at the door

SAUNDERS   For the last time, are you boys coming out or
           not?

SAM   Go away, we're busy.

SAUNDERS   Very well, then, I'm coming in.

           She enters the washroom

PETE   Have you no sense of decency?

SAUNDERS   All right, I don't know what you boys have been
           doing in here, but I want you back to work
           immediately. Pete, you've still that rug. Tom,
           there's boxes to be folded. Sam, you'd better
           get busy and sand down the edges of those
           blocks if you expect to earn anything this week.
           As for you, Jim, well, I'm beginning to have
           second thoughts.

JIM   Yes, ma'am.

           Pause. No one makes a move to go

SAUNDERS   Well, get moving!

PETE   I have to take a crap.

           He heads into one of the stalls

TOM   Me too.

           He goes into the other one

SAM   I have to use the bottle.

SAUNDERS   And how about you, Jim? Don't you have some-
           thing to do?

SAM   He has to hold the bottle for me.

SAUNDERS   He has to what, Sam?

19

SAM   Well, it's like this. I don't have a very good aim, so Princess here is gonna get down on her hands and knees...

SAUNDERS   (Cutting him off) All right, that's quite enough. When you're through here, I want you back to work. And fast. Michael, you come with me.

Michael turns around from the urinal. His pants are open, his penis exposed

MICHAEL   (To Saunders) I'm gonna disintegrate you.

SAUNDERS   (Screams) Michael! Oh, you boys, you put him up to this! Didn't you?

PETE   We did not.

SAUNDERS   Right! Mr. Carson will be here any minute. We'll see what he has to say.

She opens the door to leave

SAM   (Calling after her) Hey, be careful. He's got one too.

More screams. She exits, and is seen running down the hall. Pete and Tom emerge from the stalls laughing. Jim tidies Michael and sends him out the door

PETE   Sam, you have a warped sense of humour.

SAM   Yeah, just like the rest of me.

JIM   Proud of that, aren't you Sam? Professional cripple.

SAM   Eat shit, princess.

JIM   And such a stirling vocabulary.

Pause. Jim begins to pick up cigarette butts and matches, which by now litter the floor

TOM   Hadn't you better go before Carson gets back?

JIM   The office can wait.

TOM   What'll you do when he gets here?

JIM   I'll cross that bridge when I come to it.

TOM   Well, we'll all have to cross that bridge soon.
        We've been in here for over half an hour.

SAM   Yeah, we do tend to take long craps.

PETE   I don't care how long it takes me to crap.

        Pause

TOM   Did you get your typewriter fixed yet, Jim?

JIM   No, I haven't had time.

TOM   Well, my dad's offer still stands...If you'd
        like him to take a look at it.

JIM   Thanks, I would. How is your father?

TOM   He's okay. Why don't you bring it over Sunday?

JIM   I'll have to see. I'm kind of busy at the club.
        Christmas is coming.

TOM   It will only take an hour.

JIM   You wouldn't like to give us a hand this year,
        would you?

TOM   What did you have in mind?

JIM   I thought you might like to do our Christmas
        mural.

TOM   No, I don't think so.

JIM   Spastic Club's not good enough for chickentracks,
        eh? Seriously, Tom, I could use some help. Not
        just for the mural, but to paint posters, stuff
        like that.

TOM   How much is the Spastic Club willing to pay for
        all this?

JIM   Come on, you know there's no payment. All the
        work for the club is done on a voluntary basis.
        Carson's never paid anyone before.

SAM   So why should the old fart break his record of
        stinginess just for you?

JIM   It may interest you to know, Sam, that Carson
        doesn't get paid for his services either.

SAM   Bwess his wittle heart.

TOM   In that case, the answer's no. If I get paid
        for folding boxes, why the hell should I paint
        a lousy mural for free?

        21

JIM   I just thought it might keep you busy.

TOM   I'm busy enough.

           Jim gets up, staggers over to the waste basket
           and deposits his litter. Sam applauds

PETE   Jim, what's the Spastic Club planning for us
           boys and girls this year?

JIM   Oh, we've got a few things up our sleeve.
           Actually, we'd appreciate it if some of the
           members were a bit more co-operative. So far
           the response has been practically nil.

TOM   That's horseshit.

PETE   What about my idea of having that psychologist
           down from the university?

JIM   Well, since you're so interested, Pete, I'll
           tell you. Carson didn't think too much of it.
           He was afraid the members would be bored. I
           don't happen to agree with him, but that's the
           way he feels.

SAM   What about my idea for installing ramps in the
           subway?

JIM   It's a good idea, Sam, but that sort of thing
           doesn't come under our jurisdiction.

SAM   Who says so?

JIM   It's up to the city. We're not in a position...

TOM   Okay, Jim, what does the Spastic Club have up
           its sleeve for this year?

JIM   There's a trip to the Science Centre. One to
           the African Lion Safari. We're organizing a
           finger painting contest, that Sorority is
           throwing a Valentine's day party for us...

PETE   Wheee! A party!

           Circus music is heard low in the distance

TOM   What's the entertainment, Jim?

JIM   Puffo the Clown, Merlin the Magician...

PETE   And Cinderella, and Snow White and the Seven
           Fucking Dwarfs. Jesus Christ, Jim, Puffo the
           Clown! What do you and Carson think you're
           dealing with, a bunch of fucking babies?

Blackout, circus music at full and bright lights.
Puffo, in clown suit, has arrived, carrying
balloons. Enter also the girl and two Shriners,
the girl dressed in circus attire. She is
marching and twirling a baton. One of the
Shriners is wearing a Mickey Mouse mask and
white gloves. He follows the girl, weaving in
and around the boys, dancing in time to the
music. The other Shriner appears on a tricycle
(or on roller skates, if preferred) waving to
the audience. Puffo presents Sam, Tom and Pete
each with a balloon, and exits following the
girl and Shriners. The music fades

PETE   Who was that masked man, anyway?

On a signal from Pete, the boys burst their
balloons with their lighted cigarettes

JIM   Wait a minute, Pete, let me finish. We've got
other things planned.

PETE   Like what?

JIM   Well, for one, we're planning a trip to a glue
factory.

TOM   You're kidding.

JIM   No, I'm not. Carson thinks it might be very
educational.

TOM   What do you think, Jim? Do you think it will be
very educational?

JIM   I don't know. I've never seen them make glue
before.

PETE   Well, you take one old horse, and you stir
well...

JIM   We're planning other things too, you know.

TOM   What other things?

JIM   Well you know, theatre trips, museum trips.
These things take time, Tom. We've written
letters and...

TOM   What letters? To whom?

JIM   Letters. Lots of letters. They're at home in
my briefcase. I'll show them to you tomorrow.

TOM   Any replies?

JIM   What?

TOM   How many replies did you get to the letters?

JIM   Look, am I on trial or something?

TOM   I don't know, Jim. Are you?

JIM   Okay, maybe some of the things we do aren't as
        exciting as you and I'd like them to be, but
        I'm doing the job as well as I can, and I can't
        do it all on my own. You guys bitch about the
        program, but you won't get off your asses and
        fight for something better. That idea of Pete's
        about the psychologist, I really pushed that
        idea. Pushed it to the hilt...

PETE   But Carson didn't like it.

JIM   Carson didn't like it, and the more I pushed
        the firmer he got.

SAM   Why didn't you push it right up his ass?

JIM   (Ignoring this) So I told Pete he should go
        down and talk to Carson himself. I even made
        him an appointment. But he never showed up,
        did you, Pete?

PETE   I was busy.

TOM   Why the hell should you or Pete or anyone else
        have to beg that prick for anything?

JIM   Tom, that's not fair. So he's a little stuffy,
        at least he's interested. He does give us more
        than the passing time of day.

PETE   Sure, he was in for a whole hour this morning.

JIM   Pete, you may not like Carson, but just
        remember. If he, or the Kiwanis, or any of the
        other service clubs decide to throw in the
        towel, we're in big trouble.

SAM   "If they won't do it..."

JIM   If they won't do it, who will? You?

        A long pause

PETE   I've got nothing against the Rotary or the
        Kiwanis. If they want to give me a free meal
        just to look good, that's okay with me.

24

TOM   You're sure of that?

PETE   Tom, the Bible says the Lord provides. Right
       now He's providing pretty good. Should I get
       upset if He sends the Kiwanis instead of
       coming Himself?

JIM   If you feel like getting something, why don't
       you give something?

PETE   No, sir. I don't jump through hoops for nobody,
       and certainly not for a bastard like Carson. I
       might have nothing to say against the groups,
       but I don't have anything to say for them
       either.

TOM   You can't stay neutral all the time.

PETE   Tell that to Switzerland. Tom, you're young.
       You don't realize how tough it is for people
       like us. Baby, it's cold outside.

SAM   (Under his breath) Christ!

PETE   When I came to this dump eleven years ago, I
       wanted to be a carpenter. That's all I could
       think about ever since I can remember. But
       face it, whoever heard of a carpenter with a
       flipper like that? (Holds up his deformed hand)
       But I had a nice chat with this doc, and he
       told me I'd find what I'm looking for down here.
       So I came down here, and one of Saunders'
       flunkies shoves a bag of blocks in my hand.
       "What gives?" I said. And then it slowly dawned
       on me that as far as the doc is concerned,
       that's the closest I'll ever get to carpentry.

       And I was pissed off, sure. But then I think,
       good old doc, he just doesn't understand me.
       'Cause I still have my ideals. So in a few days
       I bust out of this place and go looking for a
       job -- preferably carpentry. What happens? I
       get nothing but aching feet and a flat nose
       from having fucking doors slammed in my face
       all the fucking time.

       And I'm at my wits end when I got a letter from
       the Spastic Club. And I said fuck that. I'm
       about to throw it in the furnace, but I get
       curious. I've heard of the Spastic Club and I
       always figured it was a load of shit. But I
       think one meeting isn't going to kill me.

So I go, and I find out I'm right. It's a load
of shit. It's a bunch of fuckheads sitting
around saying, "Aren't we just too ducky for
these poor unfortunate cripples?" But I got a
free turkey dinner.

When I got home I took a good look at myself.
I ask myself what am I supposed to be fighting?
What do these jokers want me to do? The answer
is they want to make life easier for me. Is that
so bad? I mean, they don't expect me to keep you
guys in your place or nothing. They just want me
to enjoy life. And the government even pays me
just for doing that. If I got a job, I'd lose
the pension. So why have I been breaking my ass
all this time looking for a job? And I got no
answers to that. So I take the pension, and
come back to the workshop. The only price I
gotta pay is listening to old lady Saunders
giving me hell for not weaving her goddamn rug.

Blackout. Fanfare. Lights up on far side of the
stage. The actor playing Michael enters dressed
as a freak show barker. With him is the girl,
his assistant, dressed in similar carnival
attire. The following sequence takes place in a
stage area independent of the washroom

BARKER   (To the audience) Are you bored with your job?
          Would you like to break out of the ratrace?
          Does early retirement appeal to you? Well, my
          friends, you're in luck. The Shriners, the
          Rotary, and the Kiwanis are just begging to
          wait on you hand and foot.

          Charleston music. The barker and the girl dance.
          The music continues through the next several
          speeches until he is handed the brain

          To throw you parties, picnics. To take you on
          field trips. To the flower show, the dog show,
          and to the Santa Claus Parade.

          More dancing

          Would you like to learn new skills? Like sanding
          blocks, folding boxes, separating nuts and bolts?
          My friends, physiotherapists are standing by
          eager to teach you.

The girl hands him a wooden block and another block covered with sandpaper. More dancing as he sands the block

Whoopee, is this ever fun.

He hands the block back to the girl

Now, I suppose you good people would like to know, how do I get this one-way ticket to paradise? My props, please.

The girl hands him a life-size model of a human brain which has the various sections marked off, and a hammer. The music stops. He walks downstage into a pool of light directly in front of the audience

Now all you do is take a hammer and adjust the motor area of the brain. Like this. Not too hard, now, we wouldn't want to lose you.

He taps the brain gently

Having done that, you will have impaired your muscle co-ordination, and will suddenly find that you now (Speaking with the speech defect of the character Michael) "talk with an accent". You will then be brought to our attention either by relatives who have no room for you in the attic, or by neighbors who are distressed to see you out in the street, clashing with the landscape.

Now, assuming you are successful in locating the proper point of demolition, we guarantee that this very special euphoria will be yours not for a day, not for a week, but for a lifetime. There's no chance of relapse, regression, or rehabilitation because, my friends, it's as permanent as a hair transplant. It's for keeps. Should you, however, become disenchanted with this state, there is one recourse available to you, which while we ourselves do not recommend it, is popular with many, and does provide a final solution to a very complex problem. All you do is take the hammer and simply tap a little harder.

He smashes the brain. At the moment of impact, he becomes spastic, and slowly crumbles to the floor. Blackout.

The lights come up on the four boys

SAM   Guys like you really bug me. You got two good legs and one good hand. So the other's deformed. Big Fuckin' Deal. By the way, who the hell said you couldn't be a carpenter? You had your loom fixed up in five minutes last week while that old fart of a handyman was running around town looking for something to fix it with.

PETE   That was just lucky.

TOM   You know what I think, Cochran? I think you're lazy. I think eleven years ago you were looking for a grave to fall into, and you found it in the Spastic Club.

PETE   Don't be self-righteous about things you don't understand.

TOM   I understand laziness.

PETE   You don't understand. I tried.

TOM   Aw, c'mon, Pete, you didn't try very hard.

PETE   There's no place in the outside world for a guy who talks funny.

SAM   Aw, you poor wittle boy. Did the big bad mans hurt your wittle feelings?

        Pete goes for Sam, is about to hit him, but is restrained by Tom

TOM   That's not funny, Sam. (To Pete) But it is a bit ridiculous. Here you are, you're thirty-seven years old, and you're still worried about something as small as that.

PETE   It may be a small thing to you, Tom. It's not to me.

JIM   Howdya like to have kids following you down the street calling you drunk? I get that all the time, but you learn to live with it.

SAM   Sure you learn to live with it. You learn to rub their noses in it too. Last week I was at this show and I had to be bounced about twenty steps in the chair just to get to the lobby.

28

| | Well, you know what that does to my bladder, eh? So naturally I make for the washroom. The stalls are two inches too narrow, of course. As for the urinals, I never claimed to be Annie Oakley. They don't have urinal bottles 'cause they'd fuck up the interior decoration. But then I did spy this Dixie cup dispenser... |

JIM   Sam, you didn't!

SAM   Yeah, sweetie, I did. I was just doing up my fly when the usher walked in, saw the cup sitting on the edge of the sink. He thought it was lemonade. Told me patrons weren't allowed to bring refreshments into the washroom. Then he moved closer and got a whiff.

PETE   What happened?

SAM   Another United Appeal supporter had his dreams all crushed to ratshit.

JIM   And Sam set us back another twenty years.

SAM   What do you expect me to do, Harris? Piss my pants waiting for everything to come under your jurisdiction?

PETE   Sam's right. It's like you said, Jim. You do the best with what you got.

TOM   Come on, Pete, that's a cop-out and you know it. Sam should have got rid of that cup as soon as he took his leak. Putting it on the sink in plain view of everyone, for Chrissake!

PETE   Don't be so smug. A guy survives the best way he knows how. You wait, you'll find out. They don't want us creeps messing up their world. They just don't want us.

TOM   Tough! They're going to get me whether they want me or not. I'm a man, and I've got a right to live like other men.

PETE   You're the only man I know who can make a sermon out of saying hello.

He goes into one of the stalls, slamming the door behind him

TOM   Yeah and pretty soon I'm gonna say goodbye. You expect me to spend the rest of my life folding boxes?

29

PETE   (Over the top of the stall) Look, Rembrandt,
        we know you're a great artist and all that shit.
        But if you paint like you fold, forget it.

JIM   Wait a minute, Pete. I've seen some of Tom's
        paintings. I'm no expert on abstract, but I
        think they're pretty good. They're colourful
        and...

SAM   Colourful chickentracks?

TOM   Fuck off!

JIM   Still, I'm not other people. I might like them,
        but folks on the outside might not. People get
        pretty funny when they find out something's
        been done by a handicapped person. Besides, we
        both know you can't draw.

TOM   That doesn't make any difference. I paint
        abstract.

SAM   So you'll win the finger painting contest.

JIM   Tom, we've been over this I don't know how many
        times. Name me one good abstract painter who
        isn't a good draftsman.

SAM   Name me one good writer who'd be caught dead in
        a glue factory.

JIM   Seriously, can you think of one famous artist
        who was spastic?

TOM   Jim, if you're sure I can't make it, what about
        the letter?

PETE   What letter?

JIM   (Shrugs) Oh, a letter he got from an art critic.

PETE   (Emerging from the stall) What did it say?

TOM   Here, you can read it yourself.

        He hands the letter to Pete who begins to read
        it to himself

SAM   Out loud.

        Pete starts to read it, gives up, hands the
        letter to Jim

JIM   (Reading) Dear Mr. March, I was fascinated by
        the portfolio you submitted. I cannot recall
        an artist in whose work such a strong sense of

                30

struggle was manifest, You positively stab the canvas with bold colour, and your sure grasp of the palette lends a native primitivism to your work. I am at once drawn to the crude simplicity of your figures and repulsed by the naive grotesqueries which grope for recognition in your tortured world. While I cannot hail you as a mature artist, I would be interested in seeing your work in progress this time next year.

SAM   Which one of your father's friends wrote it?

TOM   None of them.

SAM   One of your mother's friends?

TOM   The letter's authentic. I'll bring the guy's magazine column if you don't believe me.

PETE   Oh, we believe you, Tom. Critics are so compassionate.

TOM   You shit all over everything, don't you?

PETE   (Handing Tom the letter) It's a good letter, I guess.

TOM   You guess?

PETE   Well, what the hell am I supposed to say? You're the artist. I don't even like the Mona Lisa. To me she's just a fat ugly broad. But I can't help wondering, Tom...

TOM   What?

PETE   If he wouldn't have said the same thing if you'd sent him one of your boxes. (Tom starts to protest but Pete goes on) Like when I'm weaving that goddamn rug and we have visitors. Now I'm no master weaver. Matter of fact, I've woven some pretty shitty rugs in my time. But whenever we have visitors, there are always one or two clowns who come over and practically have an orgasm over my rug, no matter how shitty we both know it is.

SAM   It's the same with the blocks. They pick one up, tell me how great it is, and then walk away with a handful of splinters.

TOM   It's not the same. This guy happens to be one of the toughest art critics around.

JIM   Even tough art critics give to the United Appeal.

31

TOM   Yes, and sometimes writers write for it.

JIM   Well, it keeps me off the streets.

SAM   Yeah, Jim peddles his ass indoors where it's warm.

PETE   And Carson has an exclusive contract on it. Right Jim?

JIM   I work because I want to work. It's a challenge, I enjoy it, and I can see the results.

PETE   Sure. So can we. Hot dogs, ice cream, balloons, confetti...

JIM   Well at least I don't have illusions of grandeur.

TOM   What illusions have you got, Jim?

JIM   Tom, you've got to come down to earth sooner or later. For someone in my situation the workshop makes sense. I can be more useful in a place like this.

TOM   Useful to Carson?

JIM   No, to people like Michael and Thelma.

TOM   What about Carson? Are you going to go on kissing his ass?

JIM   Call it what you like. In dealing with people, I have to be diplomatic.

TOM   Fine, Jim. You be diplomatic for both of us.

        He gets up

PETE   Where are you going?

TOM   I'm bored. I'm leaving.

PETE   What's the matter?

TOM   Nothing, Cochran, go back and finish your shit.

JIM   Tom, what is it?

TOM   I'm quitting.

JIM   You're not serious?

TOM   Getting more serious by the minute.

JIM   You're building a lot on a few kind words, aren't you?

32

TOM	The man doesn't know I'm spastic.

TOM   The man doesn't know I'm spastic.

JIM   He's going to find out. And you know what'll happen when he does. You'll be his golden boy for a few weeks, but as soon as the novelty wears off, he'll go out of his way to avoid you.

TOM   What if the novelty doesn't wear off?

JIM   Tom, I don't think you should rush into this.

TOM   How long do I have to stay, Jim?

JIM   Stay until Christmas. Stay and do the mural.

TOM   No.

JIM   But you like painting. It won't hurt you.

TOM   I said no!

JIM   Why not?

Tom moves towards the door

JIM   Won't you at least talk about it?

TOM   (He turns and looks at Jim) That's all you know how to do now, isn't it? No writing, no thinking, just talking. Well get this straight. I don't want any part of the Spastic Club or the Workshop. It's finished, okay?

JIM   Look, I know this place isn't perfect. I agree. It's even pretty rotten at times. But, Tom, out there, you'll be lost. You're not wanted out there, you're not welcome. None of us are. If you stay here we can work together. We can build something.

SAM   Yeah, a monument to Carson. For the pigeons to shit on.

TOM   How long are _you_ going to stay here?

JIM   How long?

TOM   Are you going to spend the rest of your life being Carson's private secretary?

JIM   Well, nothing's permanent. Even I know that.

TOM   Stop bullshitting and give me a straight answer.

JIM   Okay, I'll move on. Sure.

TOM   And do what?

JIM   Maybe I'll go back to my writing.

TOM   When? (No reply) When was the last time you wrote anything?

JIM   Last month I wrote an article for "The Sunshine Friend."

PETE   (Joined by Sam) "You are my sunshine, my only sunshine..."

TOM   Shut up! I mean when was the last time you wrote something you wanted to write?

JIM   Well, you know, my typewriter's bust...

TOM   Don't give me that crap about your typewriter. You don't want to get it fixed.

JIM   That's not true...

TOM   Do you know what you're doing here? You're throwing away your talent for a lousy bit of security.

JIM   Tom, you don't understand...

TOM   You're wasting your time doing a patch up job at something you don't really believe in. (Jim does not reply. Tom moves towards him) Jim, there are stacks of guys in this world who haven't the intelligence to know where they're at. But you have. You know. And if you don't do something with that knowledge, you'll end up hating yourself.

JIM   What the hell could I do?

TOM   You could go into journalism, write a book. Listen, in this job, who can you tell it to? Spastics. Now think. Think of all the millions of jerks on the outside who have no idea of what it's really like in here. Hell, you could write a best-seller.

JIM   I've thought about it.

TOM   Well do something about it.

JIM   Don't you think I want to?

TOM   Jim, I know you're scared. I'm scared. But if I don't take this chance, I won't have a hope in hell of making it. And if you keep on doing something you don't want to do, soon you won't even have a mind. Do you think if Michael had a mind like yours he'd be content to hang around

	here all day flushing toilets?
PETE	He's right, Jim. You don't belong here. Why don't you and Tom go together?
TOM	Look, I'll help you. We can go, we can get a place, we can do it together. Come on, what do you say?

Saunders and Carson enter the hallway

SAUNDERS	They've been in here all afternoon. I tried to reason with them, but they refused to come out. I know you're busy, and I hate to bring you down here, but I'm really afraid this Rick and Stanley business is repeating itself...
CARSON	Miss Saunders.
SAUNDERS	Yes?
CARSON	Thanks, I can take it from here.

Saunders exits. Carson opens the door and stands in the doorway

| CARSON | Okay, guys, out. |

Brief pause, then Jim moves to go

TOM	Jim, how about it?
JIM	Later, Tom.
CARSON	Much later. It's time to get back to work.
TOM	I'm quitting, Carson.
CARSON	First things first. We can discuss that in the morning. (He waits) Let's go.
JIM	I'm quitting, too, sir.
CARSON	Right now I've got a good mind to fire you. Go to my office and wait for me.
SAM	He's making it real easy for you Jim. He just fired you.
CARSON	You, too, Sam. Out.
SAM	I need the bottle. Hand me the bottle, Carson.
CARSON	You've had all afternoon to use the bottle. Now, out!

35

SAM	I need the fucking bottle!
	Tom goes to get the bottle, is stopped by Carson
CARSON	You leave that bottle alone. I want you all out of here.
	Pete gets the bottle, gives it to Sam
CARSON	Pete! Goddamn it, what's wrong with you guys?
	Sam now has the bottle in his lap
CARSON	Give me that bottle! (He takes it away from Sam) Now get out of here, all of you. (Nothing happens, so he starts to wheel Sam's chair)
SAM	Take your fuckin' hands off my chair!
JIM	Listen! You never listen to me!
CARSON	For God's sake, Jim, I'll listen, but in my office.
JIM	No, here. Now!
CARSON	What's eating you?
SAM	Give me the goddamn bottle.
	He tries to get it, but Carson holds it out of his reach
CARSON	Get out of here, Sam!
	He pushes the chair away
SAM	Fucking prick!
CARSON	(Shaken) All right, what is it?
TOM	Jim, he's listening.
JIM	I don't want to spend the rest of my life here.
CARSON	Fine. You probably won't. Now can we all get back to work?
SAM	I need the fucking bottle!
TOM	Didn't you hear what he said? He said he doesn't want to spend his whole life in this dump.
CARSON	Look, March, you've been in here all the afternoon. You've got Miss Saunders all upset because

36

	of Michael, and...
SAM	<u>I need the bottle!</u>
CARSON	Shut up, Sam!
TOM	Do you know why we've been here all afternoon? Did you ever think of that?
SAM	Son of a bitch! Do you want me to piss my pants?

Carson shoves the bottle at him, Sam wheels
into the doorway of one of the stalls

TOM	Did it ever enter your head that we might think of something besides the workshop, the club, and making you look good?
CARSON	Look, I don't know what you think, and right now I really don't care. All I'm concerned with is that you get out of this washroom. If you've got a complaint, you can come and talk to me.
TOM	I won't be there. Neither will Jim.
CARSON	I said, we can discuss that in the morning. (He turns to Sam and Pete) Come on Sam, Pete, let's go.
PETE	He can't find it, Carson.
JIM	I want to be a writer.
CARSON	(To Sam and Pete) Quit fooling around, and hurry up.
JIM	I want to be a writer!
CARSON	You are a writer.
JIM	You don't understand. I want to make my living from it.
CARSON	Maybe you will, some day. But it's not going to happen overnight, is it?
TOM	If you stay here, Jim, it won't happen at all.
CARSON	It sure as hell won't if he runs off on some half-assed adventure with you.
TOM	Come on, Jim, the man's deaf.
CARSON	And what is it this time, Rembrandt? Poverty in a garret somewhere?
TOM	Better than poverty at the workshop.

37

CARSON	What are you going to paint, nude women?
TOM	You son of a bitch!
CARSON	Okay, Tom. Let's go.

He moves to usher Tom out

TOM	You fucking son of a bitch! (In pushing him off, Tom loses his balance and falls. Carson tries to help him up) Get the fuck off me, Carson! (Slowly Jim and Pete help him to his feet) Jim, you can stay and fart around as much as you like, but I'm going. Now are you with me or not?
CARSON	No, he's not. Now beat it.
TOM	Is that your answer, Jim?
JIM	Tom, wait...
TOM	I'm tired of waiting.
JIM	Maybe if I had just a little more time.
TOM	There's no time left.
JIM	Couldn't we wait till the end of the week?
CARSON	No, Jim. If you're serious about going, go now.
JIM	What about the Christmas program?
CARSON	I can find someone else.
JIM	But Christmas is the busiest time.
PETE	Go, Jim! Go with Tom!
SAM	(Overlapping) Don't let him do it to you, baby. Go!
JIM	But Tom, it's Christmas!
TOM	Jim, please!
JIM	I can't let him down now. Maybe after Christmas...
SAM	Fuck Christmas! What about Tom?
JIM	I've written all these letters, made all the arrangements...

Tom turns and moves towards the door

SAM	Piss on the arrangements! Are you going to let him walk out that door alone?

38

PETE   If you don't go now, Tom will be alone, but
            you'll be more alone. Believe me, I know.

JIM   I can't go! I can't go, Tom, because, if you
            fall, I'll be the only one there to pick you
            up. And I can hardly stand up myself.

            Tom has gone

SAM   How did you get around on campus, princess?
            Crawl on your belly? (He wheels **angrily** to the
            door) Fuckin' door! Hey, Carson, how about one
            cripple helping another?

CARSON Get him out, Pete.

            Sam and Pete exit. They wait outside the door,
            listening. Jim staggers over to the bench and
            sits

CARSON Why don't we talk about this over dinner? At my
            place, if you like.

THELMA I need a priest! Get me a priest! Someone get
            me a priest!

            Slow fade to the sound of Thelma's sobbing.
            Pete wheels Sam down the hallway. Sam is
            laughing.